FLAGS of the United States

William Crampton

GALLERY BOOKS
An imprint of W. H. Smith Publishers Inc.
112 Madison Avenue
New York, New York 10016

INTRODUCTION

The United States of America is probably unique among nations in depicting its historical growth through the changes in the design of the national flag, which shows accurately, at specific dates, the growing number of states in the Union.

In 1776 the American flag was adopted which consisted of 13 red and white stripes with the British Union Jack in the canton, each stripe representing one of the 13 colonies. In 1777 Congress adopted a flag of alternate red and white stripes with 13 white stars on a blue field. Then, in 1794, when Vermont and Kentucky were admitted, there were 15 stars and 15 stripes (the flag becoming known as the "Star Spangled Banner"), but in 1818 the decision was made to revert to the 13 stripes as emblems of the original 13 states but to show 20 stars for the then number of states. Thereafter, each time a state was added to the Union a new star was added to the flag. The most recent to be added was that of Hawaii on 4 July 1960.

The consciousness of Americans of the importance of "Old Glory" indicates a strong love of their flag, a love which is also apparent in the enthusiasm they have for state flags. In these, all 50 of which are represented in this volume, the reader will find a great variety of pictorial content, much of it depicting the homely virtues of the labor so crucial to the creation and subsequent growth of the nation.

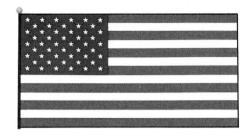

UNITED STATES OF AMERICA

Capital	Washington D.C.
Population	238,700,000
Area	3,539,289 sq miles
Largest Cities	New York, Chicago, Los Angeles, Philadelphia
National Motto	In God we trust
National Anthem	*The Star-Spangled Banner*

DISTRICT OF COLUMBIA

While not a state, the District of Columbia, a federal district of 69 square miles, was designated for Washington, the capital, and it too has its own flag. This is the banner of the arms of George Washington's family, who lived at Sulgrave Manor, a beautiful country house in Northamptonshire, England.

ALABAMA

The Cotton State

The flag of Alabama is "a crimson cross of St. Andrew on a field of white". It is usually made as a square flag, although nothing is laid down by law about its exact colors or proportions. It was created by legislation of 16 February 1895.

It is generally supposed to be modelled on the Battle Flag of the Confederacy, a flag which has also inspired several other state flags. This flag was square with a blue diagonal cross edged in white on a red field within a white border, and bearing 13 white stars. Today an oblong version of this flag, minus the white border, is usually thought of as "The Flag of the South".

Alabama also has a seal dating from 1817, and a coat of arms, adopted on 14 March 1939; this appears in the upper white triangle on the flag used by the Governor – which is otherwise like the state flag – and the state crest on the lower one. The crest is a cotton boll on a wreath in the state colors of red and white.

Alabama had a flag which was designed when the state seceded from the Union in 1861. It was blue with a picture of Liberty holding a sword and a flag. Above was the inscription *Independent now and forever*. On the reverse of the flag was a cotton plant with a rattlesnake coiled round it, and the motto *Noli me tangere* ("Don't touch me"), together with the state seal.

History	First settled by the French when part of Louisiana but ceded to Britain in 1763; in 1802 became part of Mississippi Territory. A territory in its own right in 1817, admitted to the Union on 14 December 1819. Seceded on 11 January 1861 and re-admitted in 1868
Area	51,998 sq miles
Population	(1985) 4,021,500
Capital	Montgomery
Largest City	Birmingham
Major Products	Steel, chemicals, textiles, coal, cement, stone, petroleum, cotton, poultry cattle
State Motto	We dare defend our rights
State Colors	Red and white
Bird	Yellowhammer
Tree	Southern Pine
Flower	Camellia

ALASKA

The Great Land ◆ The Last Frontier

Because Alaska is the most northerly part of the U.S.A. it is natural that its flag emblem should portray the northern stars. The two right-hand stars of the constellation of the Great Bear (the Big Dipper) point to the North Star, as portrayed on the flag. It was designed by 13-year-old Benny Benson in 1927 in the American Legion's competition to find a flag for the territory.

Without a flag, Alaska would be left out of the displays like that outside the Post Office building in Washington D.C., hence the need for a flag, although Alaska did not achieve statehood until 1959. Benny Benson's design was adopted by the legislature on 2 May 1927, and he received a reward of $1,000.

The flag was unchanged when Alaska became a state, as was the state seal adopted in 1910. The Big Dipper does not feature on the seal, but the Northern Lights do. The exact dimensions and specifications of the state flag are laid down in the 1927 legislation. The stars are to be in "natural yellow gold" and the blue is to be the same shade as the Stars and Stripes ("Old Glory Blue"). This blue is darker than in Benson's original proposal, which was to be the same shade as the state flower, the forget-me-not. The flag has the unusual proportions of width to length of 125:177, and the stars of the Big Dipper are three-fifths the size of the Polar Star, of which the diameter is one-tenth of the width of the flag.

History	Alaska lies in the extreme north-west of the American continent, facing Siberia. Settled by Russian traders from 1784 and run by the Russian-American Company, which sold it to the U.S.A. in 1867 for $7.2 million. From 1884 it was a district of Oregon; became a Territory in 1913, and admitted to the Union on 3 January 1959
Area	586,412 sq miles (the largest state)
Population	521,000
Capital	Juneau
Largest City	Anchorage
Major Products	Oil, minerals, timber, fish
State Motto	North to the future
Bird	Ptarmigan
Tree	Sitka Spruce
Flower	Forget-me-not

ARIZONA

The Grand Canyon State

In 1911 the Territory of Arizona was to be represented at the rifle shooting match in Ohio and it was felt necessary to have a flag for the team. One was designed by Colonel Charles Harris, the Territory's adjutant-general, and made up by the wife of a team member. The flag is now the state flag, since it was adopted by the state legislature in 1917, five years after Arizona became a state of the Union.

The ideas underlying Colonel Harris's design are that the red and yellow rays symbolize the period of rule by the Spaniards who gave the state its name, and also the sun setting over the desert; the copper-colored star stands for the mineral wealth, and the blue field the United States of America. Blue and yellow are now the state colors. In 1917 there were proposals for other flag designs, as not all the legislators recognized the powerful simplicity and attractiveness of Harris's design, but eventually they did agree on it, with one or two minor alterations. The battleship *Arizona* was flying this flag when it was sunk in Pearl Harbor in 1941.

Arizona also has a seal, adopted in 1910, and a wide range of other emblems. The motto, *Ditat Deus* ("God enriches") is part of the seal. A representation of the seal, 15 feet across, can be seen in the floor under the rotunda of the Capitol building in Phoenix.

History	In the south-west of the U.S.A. between the Colorado River and Mexico, and contains the Grand Canyon. First settled in 1752, when part of Mexico. Part of the huge territory ceded by Mexico to the U.S.A. in 1848. Became a Territory in 1863; admitted to the Union on 14 February 1912
Area	113,417 sq miles
Population	(1986) 3,296,000
Capital	Phoenix
Largest City	Phoenix
Major Products	Cotton, livestock, cereals, minerals (especially copper)
State Motto	*Ditat Deus* ("God enriches")
Bird	Cactus Wren
Tree	Paloverde
Flower	Saguaro cactus blossom

ARKANSAS

The Land of Opportunity

The inspiration for the design of the flag of Arkansas was almost certainly the "Flag of the South" with its star-studded diagonals, but the occasion for it was the need for a flag to present to the battleship *Arkansas*. The legislature was pressurized to adopt a flag by members of the Daughters of the American Revolution, and one of their members, Miss Willie Hocker, designed the original. According to her interpretation the 25 white stars indicate that Arkansas was the twenty-fifth state to join the Union, and the three lower blue stars stand for the first three states created from the Louisiana Purchase, of which Arkansas was one. The red, white and blue represent the Confederacy and also the Union and France, the original ruler of Louisiana. The upper blue star was added in 1924 to represent the Confederacy. The state name was added when the flag was officially approved on 26 February 1913 (so Miss Hocker's design originally had only the three blue stars in the center). The diamond is said to recall the fact that Arkansas is the only state where these gems are found. The diamond was adopted as the state gem in 1967. There is an official Pledge to the State Flag: "I salute the Arkansas Flag with its diamond and stars. We pledge our loyalty to thee." There is also a state seal, with the motto *Regnat populus* ("The people rule"), and a wide range of other emblems.

History	On river of same name, and west of the Mississippi. Was part of Louisiana territory sold to the U.S.A. in 1803 for $15 million. Area first settled in 1686; with rest of Louisiana belonged to Spain 1763-1800. Became a Territory in 1819; admitted to the Union on 15 June 1836. Seceded on 6 May 1861, and re-admitted on 22 June 1868
Area	53,187 sq miles
Population	(1984) 2,349,000
Capital	Little Rock
Largest City	Little Rock
Major Products	Bauxite and other minerals, rice, poultry, cotton, manufactured goods
State Motto	*Regnat populus* ("The people rule")
Bird	Mocking Bird (1929)
Tree	Pine (1939)
Flower	Apple blossom (1901)

CALIFORNIA

The Golden State

The Bear Flag of California, one of the best known in the U.S.A., is so-called because the picture of the grizzly bear in natural colors makes the flag very distinctive. The bear, the star, the name and red stripe are taken from the flag hoisted at Sonoma on 14 June 1846 by Americans who wanted to set up an independent republic in California, which at that time belonged to Mexico. A flag with a red star had been hoisted in 1836 by earlier Californians who wanted to break away from Mexico, so one was added to the home-made flag used at Sonoma. The grizzly bear, now extinct but once widespread in California, seemed a good symbol of strength and determination. The exact design is now unknown, since it was destroyed in the San Francisco fire on 1906. In 1911 the state legislature voted to create a flag for California which was intended to be a renewal of the 1846 flag, and the present flag was the result. The design and use of the flag are now governed by legislation of 2 June 1953.

California also has a governor's flag, which is blue with the state seal in the center in color, and a white star in each corner. This dates from 8 June 1957. The state seal was adopted in 1849 and also depicts a grizzly bear. The state has official colors – blue and gold – and a wide range of other emblems.

History	Part of the Spanish and Mexican territories. Before the war with Mexico settlers declared an independent state at Sonoma, and raised the American flag at Monterey. Became a state on 9 September 1850
Area	158,693 sq miles
Population	(1987) 27,662,900
Capital	Sacramento
Largest City	Los Angeles
Major Products	Oil, natural gas, minerals, gold, cotton, fruit, livestock, timber, fish, manufactured goods, aerospace, electronics, tourism
State Motto	I have found it (*Eureka*)
State Colors	Blue and gold
Animal	Grizzly Bear (1953)
Bird	California Valley Quail (1931)
Tree	California Redwood (1931)
Flower	Golden Poppy (1903)

COLORADO

The Centennial State ◆ The Columbine State

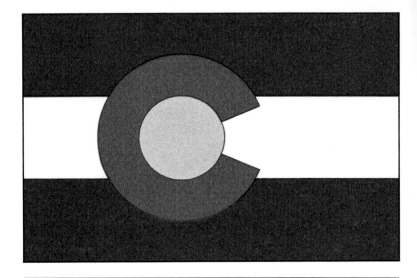

The flag normally used and illustrated for Colorado did not for many years conform to the legal specifications laid down in 1911! These made the red and yellow C much smaller than it is in practice and set right next to the staff. However, the designer actually intended it to be as we see it today. He was Andrew Carlisle Carson, whose design was approved by the legislature on 5 April 1911. He also intended the blue to be the same as that of the state flower, the columbine, but regulations of 1929 specified Old Glory Blue. Regulations of 31 March 1964 provided for the enlargement and relocation of the C.

C is for Colorado, the Columbine State, also known as the Centennial State (it entered the Union in 1876). The red and yellow recall the years of Spanish rule, and also the fact that *colorado* is the Spanish for "red". The blue and white and gold also recall the Rocky Mountain Columbine which gave the state its nickname.

The seal, adopted in 1877, carries a coat of arms and was designed by the first Territorial secretary, Lewis Ledyard Weld. It depicts several republican emblems (triangle, axe and fasces, tricolor ribbon) and a shield charged with a view of the Rockies and miners' tools, with the motto *Nil sine numine* ("Nothing without the Deity"). The first flag of Colorado, 1907-11, was blue with these arms in the center.

History	Was partly in French Louisiana and partly in Spanish (later Mexican) territory. The French part passed to the U.S.A. in 1803 and the Mexican in 1848. Became a Territory in 1861; admitted to the Union on 1 August 1876
Area	104,090 sq miles
Population	(1986) 3,267,118
Capital	Denver
Largest City	Denver
Major Products	Oil, gas, minerals, maize, wheat, potatoes, manufactured goods. Major tourist centre; 20 million visits a year
State Motto	*Nil sine numine* ("Nothing without the Deity")
Bird	Lark Bunting
Tree	Blue Spruce
Flower	Rocky Mountain Columbine

CONNECTICUT

The Nutmeg State

The emblem of Connecticut goes back to at least 1647, when it had a seal depicting vines and the motto *Sustinet qui transtulit* ("He sustains us who transplanted us"). By 1711 the vines had been reduced to three, perhaps to represent the three colonies of Connecticut, New Haven and Saybrook, and in this form appeared on the flags used in 1775 by the Connecticut militia in the Revolutionary War, which are among the oldest truly American flags. The present form of the seal was adopted on 24 March 1931 and has a slightly modified form of the motto, and the words "Seal of the Republic of Connecticut" in Latin in an oval band around the arms.

In the nineteenth century a flag of blue with the arms in the center came into use; in 1895, following pressure by members of the Daughters of the American Revolution, this became official. It was adopted by resolution on 4 July 1895 and regularized on 3 June 1897. These regulations provide for a squarish flag of blue ("azure blue") with the arms in full colour in the center. Further regulations were issued in 1957, and in practice the flag is usually made in 2:3 proportions. Like other states, Connecticut also has a distinctive flower, bird and tree. The tree, the white oak, commemorates the Charter Tree at Hartford in which the Charter of 1662 was once hidden.

History	First settled in 1634; adopted its first constitution five years later. Took over Saybrook in 1644 and New Haven in 1662, when the colony received its first Charter. Became a republican state in 1776 and ratified the U.S. constitution in 1788
Area	5,018 sq miles (third smallest state)
Population	(1983) 3,138,000
Capital	Hartford
Largest City	Bridgeport
Major Products	Manufactured goods (machinery, transportation equipment), dairy products, livestock, silage
State Motto	*Qui transtulit sustinet* ("He who transplanted sustains")
Bird	Robin (1943)
Tree	White Oak
Flower	Mountain Laurel (1907)

DELAWARE

The First State ◆ The Diamond State

The coat of arms in the center of Delaware's flag goes back to 1777, although there have been some alterations to it since then. The supporters are a farmer and a soldier, and farming is the theme of the objects on the shield (an ox, a wheatsheaf and an ear of corn). The wheatsheaf and corn were taken from the seals used by Sussex and Kent counties from at least 1683. The crest above the shield is a ship in full sail, perhaps representing the shipyards of the Delaware River. During the Civil War state troops used a flag with the coat of arms in the center (the normal system at that period), and a similar flag was presented to the battleship *Delaware* in 1910.

On 24 July 1913 the state flag was made official. The design then adopted added a diamond behind the arms, to create the colors of "colonial buff and blue", the colors of the American uniform in the Revolutionary War. The diamond shape commemorates the state's nickname. The date of ratification of the Constitution was also added to the flag.

The governor's flag is like the state flag but with a gold fringe, and a finial in the form of a Blue Hen Fighting Cock (the state bird).

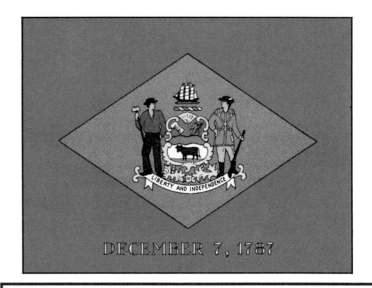

History	First settled by Dutch in 1631, then by Swedes who named it "New Sweden" (1638-55). In 1674 it passed to Britain. Was a dependency of Pennsylvania until 1776, then became a separate state. First state to ratify U.S. Constitution, on 7 December 1787
Area	2,044 sq miles (second smallest state)
Population	(1986) 633,000
Capital	Dover
Largest City	Wilmington
Major Products	Chemicals, transport equipment, processed food, livestock, corn, soybeans
State Motto	Liberty and independence
Bird	Blue Hen Fighting Cock
Tree	American Holly
Flower	Peach blossom

FLORIDA

The Sunshine State

Some five years after Alabama Florida also adopted a flag with a red saltire cross. Its original post-Civil War flag had been plain white with the state seal (6 August 1868).

The seal was adopted at the same time, but was based on one created in 1861 when Florida quit the Union. It shows a landscape with a steamboat and an Indian maiden scattering flowers. On the band is the title and the state motto "In God we trust". The red diagonal cross was added by legislation of 1899 (ratified 6 November 1900). On 8 November 1966 further legislation was passed to give the flag proportions more like those of other state flags (2:3). The red saltire, like that of Alabama, recalls the Battle Flag of the Confederacy, but it is not clear that this was necessarily the intention of the promoter of the addition, Governor Francis Fleming.

In its long history Florida has had many flags, being ruled by Spain and Britain before becoming a state of the Union. In 1845 there was a move to create a flag for the new state. It had five stripes of blue, orange, red, white and green, with the Stars and Stripes in the canton, and a scroll with the motto "Let us alone". Although this seems to have gained legal validity it was never in fact used. After secession in 1861 the armed forces were using a flag like the Stars and Stripes but with only one large star.

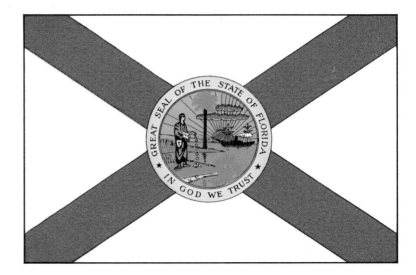

History	First permanent settlement at St. Augustine on 8 September 1565. Except for 1763-83, Florida belonged to Spain until 1821, when ceded to the U.S.A. Was a Territory until 3 March 1845, when admitted to the Union. Seceded in 1861; re-admitted in 1868
Area	58,664 sq miles
Population	(1987) 12,036,806
Capital	Tallahassee
Largest City	Jacksonville
Major Products	Citrus fruits, melons, vegetables, soybeans, sugar-cane, tobacco, fish, sea-food, metalware, timber, processed food. Tourism: 35 million tourists annually
State Motto	In God we trust
Bird	Mocking Bird (1927)
Tree	Sabal Palm (1953)
Flower	Orange blossom (1909)

GEORGIA

The Empire State of the South

Since 1879 Georgia has used state flags which deliberately recall those of the Confederacy. During the Civil War contingents of troops from Georgia used the Stars and Bars (the first flag of the Confederacy) with the state seal within the ring of stars. The 1879 flag was like this but with the stars and seal left out and the blue canton made into a vertical strip. In 1905 the state seal was added to this blue strip, and the seal was modified in 1914. The seal dates back to 8 February 1799, but in 1914 the date on it was changed from 1799 to 1776. It is the obverse side of the seal which is shown on the flag, usually in blue stitching on a white disc. The design is an allegorical one, symbolizing the three pillars of the Constitution. An official flag pledge, referring to the principles of the Constitution, was adopted in 1935.

On 1 July 1956 the present flag was adopted, in which the Bars of the old flag have given place to the whole Battle Flag of the South. This was the idea of John Sammons Bell, then chairman of the Democratic Party in Georgia, and was intended to commemorate the key role played by Georgia in the Confederacy. At the same time red, white and blue were made the state colors.

A special day each year for flying the flag in Georgia is "Georgia Day", 12 February, which commemorates its foundation in 1733.

History	Georgia lies south of Savannah River and north of Florida with an Atlantic sea-coast. Received a Charter in 1732, made a royal province in 1752. Became a state in 1776; ratified the Constitution on 2 January 1788; seceded on 19 January 1861; re-admitted on 15 July 1870
Area	58,910 sq miles
Population	(1983) 5,732,000
Capital	Atlanta
Largest City	Atlanta
Major Products	Cotton, corn, wheat, soyabeans, textiles, kaolin, wood products and paper
State Motto	Wisdom, justice and moderation
State Colors	Red, white and blue
Bird	Brown Thrasher (1935)
Tree	Live Oak (1937)
Flower	Cherokee Rose (1916)

HAWAII

The Aloha State

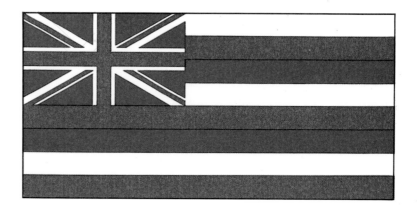

People are often surprised to find that the Union Jack still flies over part of the United States, in the canton of the flag of Hawaii. The reason is that a Union Jack was given to the King of Hawaii in 1793 by the British explorer, Captain George Vancouver, and Hawaii was under British protection from 1794-1816, and the Union Jack was its only flag. The King adopted his own flag in 1816, which had variable numbers of stripes of red, white and blue with the Union Jack in the canton. In 1845 the stripes were officially set at eight (for the eight main islands). The King and other notables also adopted arms and flags but these became obsolete when Hawaii was taken over by Americans in 1893. However, the national flag continued in use during the Republic, and after Hawaii became a Territory of the U.S.A. It became the flag of the State of Hawaii on 18 March 1959.

The present seal and coat of arms is based on those adopted by the Republic in 1896, in turn based on the royal arms of the 1850s. The modern arms depict Liberty and the figure of King Kamehameha I supporting a shield with stripes like those on the flag, and staffs known as *pululu*, emblems of protection and sanctuary. A rising sun has replaced the royal crown and a central star the religious devices. Beneath the arms is a phoenix rising from the flames. The motto is that of King Kamehameha III: *Ua mau ke ea o ka aina i ka pono* ("The life of the land is perpetuated by righteousness").

History	Pacific islands, originally inhabited only by Polynesians. First visited by Captain Cook in 1778. U.S. settlers deposed ruling Queen in 1893 and formed an independent republic. Annexed to the U.S.A. in 1898 as a Territory; admitted to the Union in 1959
Area	6,471 sq miles including 136 islands (7 inhabited)
Population	(1980) 964,691 (12.3% Hawaiians)
Capital	Honolulu
Largest City	Honolulu
Major Products	Sugar, pineapples. Tourism: about 7 million visits per year
State Motto	The life of the land is perpetuated by righteousness
Bird	*Nene* (Hawaiian goose)
Tree	*Kukui*
Flower	Hibiscus

IDAHO

The Gem State

Idaho had one seal when it was a Territory, and another after it became a state in 1890, although some of the elements from the old one were used in the new one, designed by Miss Emma Edwards in 1891. She seems to have been a partisan of women's rights, and gave a female figure, symbolic of Liberty and Justice, a prominent part on the coat of arms. The other supporter is a miner. The shield is an allegorical landscape including the River Shoshone, and is surrounded by horns of plenty, a wheatsheaf, rocks and vegetation. The crest is an elk's head and the motto *Esto perpetua* ("May it endure forever"). The star on the rim is for Idaho as a new state.

The first flag was adopted in 1907, and called for the placing of the name of the state on a blue field. In practice the seal was used as well, usually with a gold background and the arms in full color. The name appears on a red scroll beneath. The legislation of 12 March 1890 did not mention the seal but the adjutant-general of the state arranged for it to be included, and this was regularized by legislation of 15 March 1927. In 1957 Miss Edwards' actual artwork was authorized to be the official model for the seal and the flag.

Like other states Idaho also has other emblematic objects, including the Western White Pine, which appears on the arms.

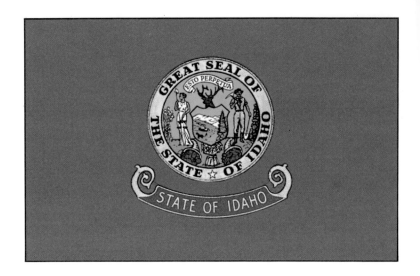

History	Idaho lies in the north-west; was once part of the Oregon Country shared between the U.S.A. and Britain (1818-48). Following the 1860 gold strike settlers and miners arrived and Idaho became a Territory in 1863. Admitted to the Union on 3 July 1890
Area	83,564 sq miles
Population	(1984) 1,001,000
Capital	Boise
Largest City	Boise
Major Products	Potatoes, wheat, timber, minerals, including silver
State Motto	*Esto perpetua* ("May it endure forever")
Bird	Mountain Bluebird (1931)
Tree	Western White Pine
Flower	Syringa (1931)

ILLINOIS

The Prairie State

The American eagle appeared on the seal of Illinois as early as 1820 when it was a Territory. Originally an eagle and shield as in the U.S. arms, the Illinois version was created when it became a state of the Union in 1818. The eagle now bears a red scroll with the legend: "State sovereignty: national union", and stands on a boulder against which a U.S shield is leaning. In 1868, when the seal was re-cut, the dates 1818 and 1868 were added to the boulder. A wreath of laurel is also part of the design, and until 1868 the eagle also grasped a bunch of arrows. A move to reverse the order of the phrases on the scroll when the seal was re-cut was defeated by special legislation, although the seal cutter evaded this to some extent by making the "national union" part more prominent. This incident was a reflection of the dissensions of the Civil War.

In 1915 the Daughters of the American Revolution ran a flag-design competition for the state, which was won by the present design produced by the Rockford chapter, and which was then presented to the legislature. On 1 July 1970 the flag was slightly revised and the name of the state was added beneath the emblem, which is now a fuller version of the contents of the seal. It includes the field, river and sunset (or possibly sunrise) from the seal.

ILLINOIS

History	Illinois is really a Mississippi valley state which also borders on Lake Michigan. First explored by the French in 1673 and belonged to French Louisiana. Part of the Indiana Territory ceded by France to Britain in 1763; conceded by Britain to the U.S.A. in 1783. Became a Territory in 1809; admitted to the Union on 3 December 1818
Area	56,400 sq miles
Population	(1985) 11,535,000
Capital	Springfield
Largest City	Chicago
Major Products	Manufactured goods, food products, coal, livestock, maize, soya beans
State Motto	State sovereignty — national union
Bird	Eastern Cardinal
Tree	Oak
Flower	Meadow Violet

INDIANA

The Hoosier State

The flag of Indiana has no relationship with the state seal, which is just as well since the seal is a very complicated one. It dates from 1801 and depicts a pioneering scene and has only been slightly revised since it first came into use. Indiana had no flag at all until 1901, when it was decided to adopt the Stars and Stripes as the state flag, a piece of legislation which has never been repealed, although it is widely ignored. In 1916 a flag-design competition was run by the Daughteers of the American Revolution to commemorate a hundred years of statehood. Their competition was won by Paul Hadley of Mooresville, and on 31 May 1917 his design was adopted by the legislature, which had seemingly forgotten the legislation of 1901.

In this flag the torch stands for liberty and enlightenment, whose rays spread far and wide. The outer ring of stars are the original 13 states and the inner ring the next five to be admitted. Above the torch is a nineteenth star for Indiana itself. In 1955 the flag was officially named the state flag (rather than "banner" as before) and is thus, in law as well as in practice, the actual state flag.

History	Similar in many ways to Illinois, and also first explored by the French. Settlements made in 1732-33; ceded to Britain in 1763 as the Indiana Territory. Became a Territory in its own right in 1800; admitted to the Union on 11 December 1816
Area	36,185 sq miles
Population	(1986) 5,503,000
Capital	Indianapolis
Largest City	Indianapolis
Major Products	Maize, wheat, oats, soya beans, coal, oil, manufactured goods
State Motto	The Crossroads of America (1937)
Bird	Cardinal (1933)
Tree	Tulip Tree (1931)
Flower	Peony (1957)

IOWA

The Hawkeye State

On the flag of Iowa only one emblem from the seal is depicted, the eagle holding a scroll (see also Illinois). Here the eagle is soaring, and the motto is "Our liberties we prize and our rights we will maintain". This dates from the seal of 1847, which also portrays a citizen soldier holding a flag with a Cap of Liberty, surrounded by objects symbolic of agriculture and industry, with the steamer *Iowa* sailing on the Mississippi. As in several other states, it was the Daughters of the American Revolution who brought up the notion of a flag and took steps to obtain a design. They won the battle for a flag in 1917, when soldiers in France were being sent copies of their state flags and the need for one for Iowa became apparent. A white flag with the eagle and scroll and name "Iowa" was used unofficially until 29 March 1921 when the present flag was adopted. One reason for this delay was that, as in Indiana, some people thought that the notion of a state flag was contrary to the ideal of national unity, as expressed by the Stars and Stripes.

The present flag has blue and red added to make a design similar to the French Tricolor. This was done at the suggestion of Mrs. Dixie Gerbhardt, a member of the D.A.R., who proposed that Iowa's origin as part of the Louisiana Purchase should be commemorated in this way.

History	Lies across the Mississippi from Illinois; until 1803 part of French Louisiana. First settled in 1788; became a Territory in 1838, the third from the Louisiana Purchase. Admitted to the Union on 28 December 1846
Area	56,275 sq miles
Population	(1984) 2,836,890
Capital	Des Moines
Largest City	Des Moines
Major Products	Corn, soya beans, livestock (especially pig-meat), coal, manufactured goods
State Motto	Our liberties we prize and our rights we will maintain
Bird	Eastern Goldfinch
Tree	Oak
Flower	Wild Rose

KANSAS

The Sunflower State

Kansas is another state whose seal depicts an allegorical landscape symbolic in this case of commerce, agriculture, the winning of the West, and the early history of the state. The motto was suggested by the Senate secretary in 1861 to explain the constellation of 34 stars; it means "To the stars through difficulties". The stars were for the states then in the Union. Kansas adopted a state flower in 1903, the wild native sunflower which has given the state its nickname. In 1925 this was placed on a flag with a state seal in the center, but with the seal so large as to obscure the sunflower, which ended up a mere gold border to the seal. On 23 March 1927 this was adopted as the state flag, with the addition of the "crest" above (a sunflower on a wreath of blue and gold). On 30 June 1963 the name "Kansas" was added below the seal, in an attempt to make the flag more distinctive.

A very distinctive flag, of blue with a large sunflower blossom was created after the adoption of this plant as the state badge. This is the state "banner" which is used as a parade flag by the National Guard, adopted as such on 30 June 1953. The same design is used as a shoulder patch by the National Guard.

History	Originally part of French Louisiana; settlement began about 1727. In 1763 ceded to Spain; in 1800 back to France; in 1803 to the U.S.A. as part of Louisiana Purchase. Became a Territory in 1854 and a state of the Union on 29 January 1861
Area	82,277 sq miles
Population	(1985) 2,450,000
Capital	Topeka
Largest City	Wichita
Major Products	Wheat, maize, sorghum, livestock, coal, oil, gas, processed food, gasoline, aircraft
State Motto	*Ad astra per aspera* ("To the stars through difficulties")
Animal	American Buffalo (1955)
Bird	Western Meadow Lark (1937)
Tree	Cottonwood (1937)
Flower	Sunflower (1903)

KENTUCKY

The Bluegrass State

"Two friends embracing" is how the statute of 1792 described the scene of the seal of the new state of Kentucky, with the motto "United we stand, divided we fall", together with the name of the state. Originally the friends stood on the edge of a precipice and wore frontier garb, but the cliff-edge has since disappeared and their costume has been upgraded. The name is now on the rim of the seal, which also bears a sprig of goldenrod, the state flower.

During the Civil War Kentucky, like other Union states, used a blue flag with its seal or arms in the center, and such a flag was made official for the National Guard in 1880. On 26 March 1918 the state legislature voted for the adoption of a flag, but it was not until 1928 that a model was actually created – a drawing of it was incorporated into the statutes. An adaptation of the state seal appears in the center (the motto is not on a scroll as it is in the seal, nor is the rim of the seal included). The name appears in an arc above, and an enlarged version of the sprig of goldenrod below. This was regularized in legislation of 14 June 1962, which also provides for a distinctive finial to the flagstaff, a Kentucky Cardinal "in an alert but restful pose."

History	Kentucky lies west across the Appalachians from Virginia. First settled from there in 1765 and was in effect a colony of Virginia until it achieved statehood in its own right on 1 June 1792 (the second to do so after the original 13)
Area	40,409 sq miles
Population	(1986) 3,728,000
Capital	Frankfort
Largest City	Louisville
Major Products	Coal, oil, gas, tobacco, corn, livestock, machinery, tourism
State Motto	United we stand, divided we fall
Animal	Grey Squirrel (1968)
Bird	Kentucky Cardinal (1926)
Tree	Kentucky Coffee Tree (1976)
Flower	Goldenrod (1926)

LOUISIANA

The Pelican State

The pelican emblem of Louisiana dates back to at least 1812 when it was used on the state seal, but no picture of this remains. On 26 January 1861 the Pelican Flag was adopted when the state seceded from the Union, but again the exact form is not known: it was captured by Admiral Farragut in 1862. Another state flag was adopted in February 1851, of blue, white and red stripes with a blue canton containing a yellow star. This remained the state flag until the end of the Civil War. Rival seals were used by the Federal and Confederate governors in 1864. The word "Union" from the motto was put first in the Federal seal and "Justice" in the Confederate one.

In 1902 a new state seal was created using the pelican emblem, the pelican of heraldry rather than of natural history. The heraldic pelican is always shown tearing its own breast to feed its young, as here, where it has three youngsters in its nest. In European heraldry the pelican in this form represents piety and self-sacrifice. Around it is the motto "Union, justice and confidence". On 1 July 1912 the flag was adopted, which bears the pelican in its nest as on the seal, with the motto on a scroll beneath. The brown pelican became the state bird in 1966.

History	Before 1803 Louisiana was the name of the whole territory drained by the river and its tributaries. Claimed for France in 1682; ceded to Spain in 1763; back again in 1800; and to the U.S.A. in 1803. Modern Louisiana became a Territory in 1804 and state on 30 April 1812. Seceded on 26 January 1861; re-admitted in July 1868
Area	52,453 sq miles
Population	(1985) 4,481,000
Capital	Baton Rouge
Largest City	New Orleans
Major Products	Oil, gas, sulphur, salt, wood products, corn, livestock, sugar-cane, rice
State Motto	Union, justice and confidence
Bird	Pelican
Tree	Bald Cypress
Flower	Magnolia

MAINE

The Pine Tree State

When Maine became a state in 1820 it adopted a seal which included a coat of arms. The main feature of the shield is a pine tree commemorating the white pines used for shipbuilding in earlier centuries, a source of wealth for the area. The moose is another well-known product. Above the shield is the North Star, with the motto *Dirigo* ("I direct"), a reference to Maine being then the most northerly state. The supporters are a farmer and a sailor. The seal does not include a rim with an inscription, as is usual elsewhere, so it is in effect a coat of arms on a circular landscape. The design is credited to Benjamin Vaughan of Hallowell. During the Civil War Maine like other Union states used its arms on a blue flag for its militia.

On 21 March 1901 Maine adopted another flag, of buff with a large pine tree in the center and the North Star in blue in the canton. This is still valid, but in practice is not in use. On the other hand, on 24 February 1909 the former militia flag was officially adopted as the state flag. It is still in the form of a militia flag, with 26:33 proportions, fringe, cord and tassels, etc.

On 21 July 1939 Maine adopted a third flag, of white with a pine tree and with an anchor behind it; above is the motto *Dirigo* and below the name "Maine", both in blue. This is the "merchant and marine" flag which is used at sea.

History	In the extreme north-east of the U.S. surrounded on three sides by Canadian territory. First settlement established in 1623. Belonged to Massachusetts from 1652 to 1820. Became a state in its own right on 15 March 1820
Area	33,265 sq miles
Population	(1986) 1,174,000
Capital	Augusta
Largest City	Portland
Major Products	Potatoes, dairy products, eggs and poultry, timber and wood products, fish and seafood, paper. Tourism: about 4 million visitors annually
State Motto	*Dirigo* ("I direct")
Bird	Chickadee (1927)
Tree	White Pine (1945)
Flower	White Pine cone and tassel (1895)

MARYLAND

The Old Line State

Like Louisiana Maryland has a very heraldic flag, which like the seal derives from the arms of the Lords Proprietors of the seventeenth century. Sir George Calvert, later Lord Baltimore, received a charter in 1632, and used his arms in a seal. His grandmother was a Crossland so he inherited those arms, which also appear in the seal. This was in use until 1776, and was revived in 1876 for the state of Maryland. The reverse shows the quartered shield of Crossland and Calvert as on the modern state flag, with supporters, crown, helmet, a motto on a scroll and another motto around the rim. The obverse of the seal is a picture of a medieval knight on horseback in the Crossland-Calvert panoply with Lord Baltimore's title around the rim in Latin. The then state seal was used on a blue flag at the time of the Civil War, but afterwards there was a move to restore the old Crossland-Calvert emblems. The quartered banner of arms was first used by the governor in 1901, and adopted as the state flag in 1904.

The Calvert arms are, heraldically described, *paly of six or and sable, a bend counterchanged*, i.e. six vertical strips of yellow and black with a counterchanged diagonal. The Crossland arms are: *quarterly argent and gules a cross bottonée counterchanged* i.e. white and red quarters with a counterchanged cross with buttons at the end of the arms. The cross's arms originally ended in *fleurs de lis*.

History	In 1767 Mason and Dixon established its boundary with Pennsylvania on a famous line. The Proprietors ruled Maryland until 1776 when the state was formed. It ratified the U.S. Constitution on 28 April 1788
Area	10,460 sq miles
Population	(1986) 4,463,000
Capital	Annapolis
Largest City	Baltimore
Major Products	Dairy products, poultry, coal, cement, electrical and electronic equipment, processed food, tourism
State Motto	*Scuto bonae voluntatis Tuae coronasti nos* ("With the shield of thy goodwill Thou hast covered us")
Bird	Baltimore Oriole
Tree	White Oak
Flower	Black-eyed Susan

MASSACHUSETTS

The Bay State

The arms and flags of Massachusetts are among the oldest in the United States. Its flag of 1776 of white with a pine tree and the motto "Appeal to Heaven" was widely used during the Revolutionary War, although less so afterwards. Its militia flag of 1787 was also white, and bore the state arms on the obverse, and on 18 March 1908 this flag became the official state flag, with a reverse side showing a green pine tree on a blue shield. This often had the crest from the arms as well, and a motto scroll without a motto. On 31 October 1971 the reverse was made identical with the obverse. The governor's flag is a triangular version of the state flag, with a gold fringe.

Massachusetts had a seal as early as 1629, although it was not in use after 1684. In 1780 a new one was designed, which in effect is a coat of arms. The Indian from the old seal is on a blue shield with a star representing the U.S.A., with a crest of a hand holding a sword. This is referred to in the motto *Ense petit placidam sub libertate quietem* ("By the sword we seek peace, but peace only under liberty"). On the seal the arms are surrounded by a rim with the title "Seal of the Republic of Massachusetts" in Latin.

On 1 November 1971 Massachusetts readopted its maritime flag. This is like the 1776 flag but does not have the inscription.

History	First settled by the Pilgrim Fathers in 1620; Colony formed in 1628 and played a leading part in the Revolutionary War (Maine has since been detached). Massachusetts ratified the Constitution on 6 February 1788
Area	8,284 sq miles
Population	(1984) 5,741,000
Capital	Boston
Largest City	Boston
Major Products	Dairy products, poultry, fruit and vegetables, timber, fish and sea-food, electrical and electronic equipment, and machinery.
State Motto	*Ense petit placidam sub libertate quietem* ("By the sword we seek peace, but peace only under liberty")
Bird	Chickadee
Tree	American Elm
Flower	Mayflower

MICHIGAN

The Wolverine State

The seal of Michigan also contains, in effect, a coat of arms. They were designed by Lewis Cass, governor of the Territory, on the basis of the arms of Hudson's Bay Company, and adopted on 2 June 1835. On the shield is a figure standing on the lake shore and the word *Tuebor* ("I will defend"). The supporters are an elk and a moose; the crest is an American eagle bearing an olive branch and a bunch of arrows, as on the arms of the U.S.A., and it also has the same motto *E pluribus unum* ("Out of many, one"). Beneath the shield is another motto: *Si quaeris peninsulam amoenam circumspice* ("If you are seeking a pleasant peninsula – look around you"). This refers to the main geographical feature of Michigan, so perhaps peninsula should be plural. This motto is said to be copied from the memorial to Sir Christopher Wren in St. Paul's Cathedral. On the seal the arms are surrounded by a rim with the title and the date AD MDCCCXXXV (1835).

The first Michigan flag was displayed in 1837 and used the seal. Later flags added the coat of arms to a blue field. Such a flag was used on Independence Day 1865 when the governor dedicated the war memorial at Gettysburg; this one had the U.S. arms on the reverse. In 1911 the flag with the state arms on both sides was adopted. The governor's flag is the same, but on a white field, so the arms are much easier to distinguish than on the state flag.

History	Michigan consists of two peninsulas between Lakes Superior, Michigan and Huron. Originally French, settled in 1668 and ceded to Britain in 1763. Part of the Indiana Territory, and conceded to the U.S.A. in 1783, became a Territory in 1805, a state on 26 January 1837
Area	58,527 sq miles
Population	(1986) 9,145,000
Capital	Lansing
Largest City	Detroit
Major Products	Transport equipment, machinery, cement, chemicals, furniture, paper, maize, oats, livestock, tourism
State Motto	*Tuebor* ("I will defend")
Bird	Robin (1931)
Tree	White Pine (1955)
Flower	Apple blossom (1897)

MINNESOTA

The North Star State ◆ The Gopher State

Minnesota was once the most northerly state of the Union, hence the nickname, and it was when the seal was designed in 1858. The central disc is another allegorical landscape, which in this case expresses the idea of the former wild and Indian country being settled by farmers. The ribbon bears the name of the North Star in French, a reminder that the area was first explored by the French. On the flag of the state militia the seal on a white ground was surrounded by 18 stars together with the North Star, signifying that Minnesota was the nineteenth state to join the Union after the original 13. The reverse was blue. On 4 April 1893 this was adopted as the state flag, with some differences, e.g. the seal was back to front (its original official form), was decorated with flowers and ribbons with the dates 1819 and 1893 (the date of the establishment of Fort Snelling and the date the flag was adopted), and the name of the state was written below. The date of statehood, 1858, was placed above the disc. The reverse of the flag was plain blue.

On 19 March 1957 the flag was thoroughly revised. It is now blue on both sides, the seal is the right way round and in color, and is surrounded by moccasin flowers, the state flower; the seal, the 19 stars and the name are now on a white disc edged in yellow. A campaign is currently under way to revise the flag completely.

History	Explored by the French in the 1650s and claimed by France. Divided between Britain and Spain in 1763. The Spanish part became American by the Louisiana Purchase; the British part was conceded in 1783. Organized as a Territory in 1849; became a State on 11 May 1858
Area	84,402 sq miles
Population	(1986) 4,214,013
Capital	St. Paul
Largest City	Minneapolis
Major Products	Iron ore and other minerals, sugarbeet, sweet corn, wheat, dairy products, mink, turkeys, cattle, wild rice, timber, machinery
State Motto	L'etoile du Nord ("Star of the North")
Bird	Common loon
Tree	Red Pine
Flower	Moccasin flower

MISSISSIPPI

The Magnolia State ◇ The Bayou State

The Battle Flag of the Confederacy still flies high in Mississippi, where it was made part of the state flag in 1894, the other part of the flag being an adaptation of the Stars and Bars. The committee report which recommended and described this design did not actually designate the Battle Flag by name, but there is no doubt of the intention. The report also stipulated that the finial of the flagstaff should be in the form of an axehead and spear.

When it seceded from the Union the state used the Bonnie Blue Flag (a blue flag with a large white star) which had previously been used in the Republic of West Florida in 1810 when Americans tried to detach the area from Spanish rule. There was also an earlier flag, the one used by Nathan and Kemper in the rebellion of 1804. This had seven blue and white stripes and a red canton with two white stars, clearly based on the Stars and Stripes. In 1861 there was another state flag, of white with a magnolia tree (now the state tree), and the Bonnie Blue Flag in the canton.

The Mississippi coat of arms is based on the seal, which in turn is derived from that of the U.S.A. The eagle holds six arrows rather than 13, and is on a blue shield with the name above it. Below the shield are stalks of cotton and a ribbon with the motto *Virtute et armis* ("By valor and arms"). The seal was adopted in 1817. Neither was used in the period of 1861-70.

History	The French set up the first settlements but ceded the area to Britain in 1763; conceded to the U.S.A. in 1783. Became a Territory in 1798, and a state in 1817. Seceded 1861; re-admitted in 1870
Area	47,689 sq miles
Population	(1985) 2,656,600
Capital	Jackson
Largest City	Jackson
Major Products	Cotton, soya beans, rice, corn, timber and wood products. Tourism: about 1.5 million visits per year
State Motto	*Virtute et armis* ("By valor and arms")
Animal	White-tailed Deer (1974)
Bird	Mocking Bird (1944) Waterfowl – Wood Duck (1974)
Tree	Magnolia (1938)
Flower	Magnolia (1952)

MISSOURI

The Show Me State

Missouri's origin as part of French Louisiana is clearly demonstrated in its flag, based on the French Tricolor (see also Iowa). The flag was designed by one of the Daughters of the American Revolution, whose husband submitted it to the state legislature in 1909. It was rejected twice before finally being accepted on 22 March 1913. Here also there was a rival move to adopt the Stars and Stripes as the state flag.

In the center of the flag is the state seal with the outer rim occupied by a ring of 24 stars, which tell us that the state was the twenty-fourth to join the Union. These stars also appear above the arms in the seal, which dates from 11 January 1822. The arms have three quarters, one with the United States arms, one with a grizzly bear and one with a crescent moon. The crescent, the heraldic sign of a second son, signifies that Missouri was the second state formed from the Louisiana Purchase. The supporters are also grizzlies. Around the shield is a belt with the motto "United we stand, divided we fall" (see also Kentucky); below is a scroll with another motto: *Salus populi suprema lex esto* ("Let the welfare of the people be the supreme law"). Beneath this is the date MDCCCXX (the date of the Missouri Compromise which allowed the territory to join the union).

History	Missouri was the "launching pad" for the Winning of the West. First settled by the French in 1735; ruled by Spain (1763-1800); sold to the U.S.A. as part of the Louisiana Purchase. Was the second Territory formed from the area (1812); became a state on 10 August 1821
Area	69,697 sq miles
Population	(1986) 5,066,000
Capital	Jefferson City
Largest City	St. Louis
Major Products	Lead, zinc, coal, corn, soya beans, wheat, transport equipment
State Motto	*Salus populi suprema lex esto* ("Let the welfare of the people be the supreme law")
Bird	Bluebird (1927)
Tree	Flowering Dogwood (1955)
Flower	Hawthorn (1923)

MONTANA

The Treasure State

Montana's flag is based on the colors carried by the state militia in the Philippine Campaign of 1898, which were a blue flag of the usual military dimensions with the state seal in the center and inscriptions. On 27 February 1905 it was voted to make this the state flag, with the state seal only on the blue field.

The seal was adopted in 1865 when Montana was still a territory, re-adopted in 1893 and revised in 1935. It is another allegorical landscape, based on a view of the Great Falls of the Missouri and the Rocky Mountains, with mining and agricultural implements in the foreground. Originally buffalo and other animals were also to be seen. The scroll bears the words *Oro y plata* ("Gold and silver") which refers not only to the mining industry but also to the period when the area was, in name at least, subject to Spain. No official colors were designated for the seal.

In 1981 the seal as used on the flag was given official colors in terms of the Pantone Matching System, and the flag was revised by adding the name of the state in gold block letters beneath the seal, and by moving from military dimensions to the more usual flag proportions. The new style flag was introduced on 1 October 1981.

History	Montana lies mostly on the eastern side of the Rocky Mountains which give it its name. Became part of the U.S.A. with the Louisiana Purchase; sparsely settled until the gold strikes of the 1860s. Became a Territory in 1864 and a State on 8 November 1889
Area	147,138 sq miles
Population	(1986) 819,000
Capital	Helena
Largest City	Billings
Major Products	Oil, copper and other minerals, wheat, tourism
State Motto	*Oro y plata* ("Gold and silver")
Bird	Western Meadowlark
Tree	Ponderosa Pine
Flower	Bitter-root

NEBRASKA

The Cornhusker State

The seal of Nebraska is another which contains an allegorical scene which it could be hard to distinguish from others shown on state flags. It dates from 1867 and was designed by a member of the House of Representatives, Isaac Wiles. The scene depicts "the mechanic arts" (the blacksmith at his anvil), agriculture, transport by rail and river and the Rocky Mountains in the background. The motto is "Equality before the law".

During the First World War the seal was added to unofficial flags sent out to soldiers, and after the war the Daughters of the American Revolution pressured the legislature to adopt a flag officially. The design they had in view was a blue flag with a revised state seal and a sprig of goldenrod, the state flower, in the canton, but they had no success until 2 April 1925 when approval was gained for the use of a blue flag with the (unchanged) state seal in gold. This was first hoisted over the University of Nebraska football stadium in that year. It was finally officially adopted in 1963.

Since 1931 there has been a hymn to the flag, the "Flag Song of Nebraska", written by Mrs. B.G. Miller who was a leader of the flag campaign of 1925, with music by George H. Aller.

History	Nebraska is one of the leading agricultural states. First explored by Coronado in 1541 and later became part of French Louisiana. Then sold to the U.S.A. (1803); began to be settled (1847); in 1854 it became a Territory. Admitted to the Union on 1 March 1967
Area	77,355 sq miles
Population	(1985) 1,605,574
Capital	Lincoln
Largest City	Omaha
Major Products	Maize, wheat, sorghum, cattle, oil
State Motto	Equality before the law
Bird	Western Meadowlark (1929)
Tree	American Elm
Flower	Goldenrod (1895)

NEVADA

The Silver State

Nevada also has an allegorical scene-type seal, but this does not now appear on the flag of the state. The flag now in use, adopted on 26 March 1929, is based on the winning entry in a design competition run by the government. The prize of $25 for the best entry went to Louis Shellback, but before being adopted his design had the name Nevada added around the points of the star. The motto "Battle Born" was intended to signify the fact that Nevada achieved statehood (represented by the single white star) during the Civil War. The state flower, the sagebrush, forms a wreath around the star.

The seal did appear in the center of the previous flag, adopted on 22 March 1915, in the form of an ornate shield, with the name above in white and the motto "All for our Country" below in yellow, all surrounded by two arcs of eighteen stars, the upper one yellow and the lower one white. In practice this flag was never very widely used, although one copy was presented to the battleship *Nevada*. An earlier flag, authorized on 25 February 1905 had the name Nevada in large letters in the center, 36 stars of yellow and white, two large white stars, and the words "Silver" and "Gold" in their respective colors (see also Montana). The 36 stars referred to the fact that Nevada was the thirty-sixth state to join the Union.

History	Originally part of Mexico Nevada was ceded to the U.S.A. in 1848 and was at first attached to Utah. Gold was found in 1859, and in 1861 it became a Territory. Joined the Union on 31 October 1864
Area	110,561 sq miles
Population	(1986) 1,007,850
Capital	Carson City
Largest City	Las Vegas
Major Products	Gold, oil, silver, cattle, hay, potatoes
State Motto	All for our country
Animal	Bighorn sheep (1973)
Bird	Mountain Bluebird
Tree	Single-leaf Piñon (1959)
Flower	Sagebrush (1959)

NEW HAMPSHIRE

The Granite State

The New Hampshire seal is more pictorial than most, depicting the building of a sailing ship on the stocks at Portsmouth. The ship is supposed to be the *Raleigh*, one of the first vessels of the U.S. Navy, launched in 1776. The flag she is flying is therefore incorrect, since it was not adopted until a year later. Around this scene is a wreath of laurel. The seal was adopted in 1784 and redrawn in 1931, when the date "1776" was substituted for the original "1784".

A blue flag with the seal was used as early as 1792 for the state troops and remained as a purely military flag until 24 February 1909 when the design was adopted as the state flag, with a further wreath of laurel interspersed with nine stars around the seal, all in yellow. On 1 January 1932 the modified seal was substituted. A move in 1944 to replace the flag with a better design failed.

New Hampshire also has a state emblem, adopted on 3 May 1945. It is an oval with a view of a strange rock formation called the "Old Man of the Mountains". On the rim is the name "State of New Hampshire" and the motto "Live free or die". The original motto of the state was *Vis unita fortior* ("United strength is greater"). This appeared on the seal of 1775 but not on the present seal, adopted in 1784.

History	The state lies between Massachusetts Bay and Canada. Inland are the granite-based mountains that give it its nickname. Area was first settled in 1623 at Rye; became a separate province in 1679. An independent state government was set up in 1776, and the state ratified the U.S. Constitution on 21 June 1787
Area	9,279 sq miles
Population	(1985) 998,000
Capital	Concord
Largest City	Manchester
Major Products	Hay, vegetables, apples, livestock, machinery, metalware, stone
State Motto	Live free or die
Bird	Purple Finch
Tree	White Birch
Flower	Purple Lilac

NEW JERSEY

The Garden State

As in the other original 13 states the seals and other trappings of the royal government were done away with in 1776 in favour of republican ones. A new seal for New Jersey was created by Eugene de Simitière, based on a coat of arms. This has a blue shield with three ploughs in natural colors. The supporters are figures of Ceres, goddess of agriculture, and Liberty. The crest is a horse's head. All these details were laid down by the supervising committee, but other features were added by the artist, including the date MDCCLXXVI.

In 1928 the details of the seal were regularized, including the colors of the coat of arms. A ribbon with the names "Liberty and prosperity" (referring to the supporters of the arms) and the date in arabic figures was added at this time. On 26 March 1898 the arms were placed on a buff ground to make a flag for the governor as commander-in-chief of the state troops. The buff was derived from the flag ordered for the armed forces on 28 February 1780, which was to be in the same color as facings of the uniform coat. The legislation erred in supposing that the buff was in turn derived from the flag of the Netherlands, which had once colonized the area. In 1938 the use of the governor's flag was extended to the general public, although in fact it had already passed into widespread use.

History	Has strong industrial activity and extensive agricultural base. First settled by the Dutch in 1623. Became an English colony in 1664, and a royal province in 1702. Independent government was set up in 1776 and the state ratified the Constitution on 18 December 1787
Area	7,787 sq miles
Population	(1985) 7,562,000
Capital	Trenton
Largest City	Newark
Major Products	Chemicals, electronic and electrical equipment, machinery, tomatoes, corn, fruit
State Motto	Liberty and prosperity
Bird	Eastern Goldfinch (1935)
Tree	Red Oak
Flower	Purple Violet

NEW MEXICO

The Land of Enchantment

New Mexico has one of the most distinctive and attractive flags of any of the fifty states, and one which ably reflects the history and nature of the state. The colors of red and yellow recall the era of Spanish rule (c.1600-1821). The emblem is the Zia Indian symbol of the sun, which is described in the state flag pledge as "the Zia symbol of perfect friendship among united cultures". The flag was designed by Dr. Harry Mera, an archaeologist, and was adopted with the help of members of the Daughters of the American Revolution on 15 March 1925. The Zia symbol is also the origin of the layout of the state Capitol building.

Before 1925 New Mexico had another flag, of light blue with the Stars and Stripes in the canton and the name "New Mexico" in white letters. The number 47 (referring to its order of admission to the Union) was in the upper fly and the state seal in the lower fly. The state seal was adopted on 1 February 1887 and readopted on 15 March 1913, after New Mexico had become a state. It combines the eagles of the U.S.A. and Mexico, symbolizing the cession of New Mexico to the U.S.A in 1848.

History	The state lies around the headwaters of the Rio Grande. Name was originally applied to all the northern part of Mexico which was lost to the U.S.A. in 1848. Became a Territory in its own right in 1850, although Utah and Arizona were later separated off, other areas were lost to Texas and Colorado. Became the forty-seventh state in 1912
Area	121,335 sq miles
Population	(1987) 1,500,000
Capital	Santa Fé
Largest City	Albuquerque
Major Products	Uranium and other minerals, oil, gas, cereals, cotton, livestock
State Motto	*Crescit eundo* ("It grows as it goes")
Bird	Roadrunner
Tree	Piñon
Flower	Yucca flower

NEW YORK

The Empire State

The arms of New York, which have appeared on its flags since at least 1778, were first designed in 1777, although they have been revised in minor ways since then. The shield depicts the sun rising over a maritime scene. The shield is supported by Liberty and Justice. The motto is *Excelsior* ("Ever higher"), and the crest is an eagle surmounting a globe. An official depiction of the arms was created in 1882.

The flag used in the Revolutionary War had the arms on a blue field. In 1858 the same flag with a white field was laid down for the state militia. On 8 April 1898 the field was changed to buff, like that of New Jersey, and for the same reason – it was the color of the facings in the American uniform. However, on 2 April 1901 the field was changed back to blue and has remained so ever since.

New York's governor uses the same flag with a white star in each corner – the four stars of a commander-in-chief. He has a chief-of-staff (the adjutant-general) who also has a flag. This has the crest from the arms flanked by the two white stars of a major-general, and its field color varies with the arm of the service from which the officer is seconded, i.e. red for the Army, dark blue for the Navy, light blue for the Air Force.

History	Henry Hudson (after whom its chief river is named) claimed the area for the Dutch in 1609. The first colonists arrived in 1624. In 1644 the colony was taken over by Britain. Independence was declared on 20 April 1777, and the state ratified the Constitution on 26 July 1788
Area	49,108 sq miles
Population	(1985) 17,783,000
Capital	Albany
Largest City	New York City
Major Products	Dairy products, maize, wheat, fruit, maple syrup, titanium and other minerals, clothing, machinery, processed foods
State Motto	*Excelsior* ("Ever higher")
Bird	Bluebird
Tree	Sugar Maple
Flower	Rose

NORTH CAROLINA

The Tar Heel State ◆ The Old North State

North Carolina adopted a flag as soon as it seceded from the Union. The first resolution to create one was passed on 20 May 1861, although the original design was passed over in favour of one like the present one with the red and blue transposed. On the red strip was a star and the dates "May 20th 1775" and "May 20th 1861". The first of these is that of the supposed declaration of independence at the town of Mecklenburg. This flag was adopted on 22 June, 1861, and is in the colors of the Stars and Bars, the Confederate flag adopted in March of that year.

On 9 March 1885 the design of the flag was revised. The blue and red were transposed, the width of the vertical strip reduced, and the date "April 12th 1776" inscribed below the star in place of the 1861 date. It refers to the passing of the "Halifax Resolves" which empowered the state's delegates to vote for independence. The letters N C were added flanking the star. On 9 March 1909 legislation was passed to encourage the wider use of the flag.

North Carolina has a seal which does not appear on any flag. Although revised in modern times its basis goes back to 1776. It depicts the figures of Liberty and Prosperity and contains the state motto: *Esse quam videri* ("To be rather than to seem"). The state colors are red and blue, as in the flag.

History	First English permanent settlement was in 1653. The Colony of North Carolina created in 1712; declared its independence in 1776. Ratified the Constitution on 21 November 1789; seceded on 20 May 1861. Was re-admitted to the Union in 1868
Area	52,669 sq miles
Population	(1986) 5,874,429
Capital	Raleigh
Largest City	Charlotte
Major Products	Tobacco, maize, soya beans, textiles, furniture, mica, minerals, timber
State Motto	*Esse quam videri* ("To be rather than to seem")
Animal	Gray Squirrel (1969)
Bird	Cardinal (1943)
Tree	Pine (1963)
Flower	Dogwood (1941)

NORTH DAKOTA

The Flickertail State

North Dakota's flag is a pure military color. The regimental color of the U.S. Army was like this in the 1890s, with inscriptions. A similar flag was carried by the First North Dakota Infantry in the Philippine Campaign, 1898-99, and their battalion commander, Major John Fraine, promoted in the legislature a bill to make the Color the state flag. This was enacted on 3 March 1911, although the flag as described in the legislation was not exactly the same as the Color. In 1943 the law was changed to correct this error. The flag proved to be inappropriate for the state's National Guard, since it was so like a regulation Color, and so on 15 March 1957 the legislature approved a coat of arms which could be used by them on a flag. The arms are depicted a green flag, and consist of a yellow shield shaped like a Sioux arrowhead, with a green diagonal on which are three stars, and with a fleur de lis. The crest is a bow and three arrows, and the motto on a scroll beneath is "Strength from the soil". The governor's flag is like this with a white star in each corner.

The bow and three arrows also appear on the seal adopted in 1889, which is of the allegorical-landscape type, also containing 42 stars – the number of states in the Union at the time North Dakota was admitted.

History	The Dakota Territory was part of the Louisiana Purchase in 1803, with the Red River valley ceded by Britain in 1818. First settled in 1819, became a Territory in 1861; in 1889 was divided into two states. North Dakota admitted to the Union on 2 November 1889
Area	70,665 sq miles
Population	(1984) 686,000
Capital	Bismarck
Largest City	Fargo
Major Products	Barley, sunflowers, flaxseed, durum, wheat, oil, gas, cattle
State Motto	Liberty and union, now and forever, one and inseparable
Bird	Western Meadowlark
Tree	American Elm
Flower	Wild Prairie Rose

OHIO

The Buckeye State

The state tree, the buckeye, gave the state its nickname, and also suggested (from the shape of its seed) the O in the state flag. The flag is a very distinctive one: it is the only one of the 50 which is not rectangular. It is in fact based on the cavalry pennon of the 1862-85 period, and was designed by John Eisenmann in 1901. The legislature adopted the design as the state flag on 9 May 1902, following its use at the Pan-American Exposition at Buffalo, N.Y.

Eisenmann described the flag as representing the landscape of Ohio with its roads and waterways, and the O as standing for Ohio as well as for the buckeye. The 17 stars indicate that Ohio was the seventeenth state to join the Union.

The seal of Ohio is of the allegorical landscape variety, depicting the sun rising over Mount Logan and the Scioto River, and was adopted in 1868 and revised in 1967 to incorporate the new state motto adopted on 1 October 1959: "With God all things are possible". This appears on a scroll beneath the seal. Since 1905 the state governor has had a flag of red with the state seal in the center. Around this is a ring of 13 stars, with four further stars, one in each corner. Some versions of this flag have the motto on a scroll as well as the seal.

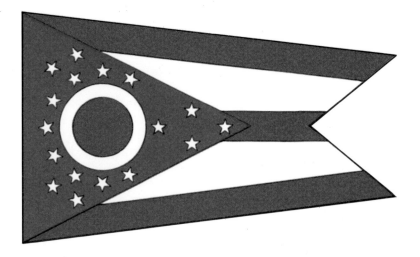

History	Settlers first arrived in area in 1788, and it was part of the Territory conceded to the U.S.A. in 1783. Was then part of the North-West Territory; became a state on 1 March 1803 (a date fixed retroactively in 1953)
Area	41,330 sq miles
Population	(1985) 10,744,000
Capital	Columbus
Largest City	Cleveland
Major Products	Coal, oil, gas, maize, wheat, oats, non-electrical machinery, transport equipment
State Motto	With God all things are possible
Bird	Red Cardinal (1933)
Tree	Buckeye (1953)
Flower	Scarlet Carnation (1904)

OKLAHOMA

The Sooner State

Oklahoma is fortunate in having a very distinctive flag, thanks to the efforts of the local Daughters of the American Revolution who secured its adoption on 2 April 1925. Their design competition was won by Mrs. Luise Fluke, with the aid of Dr. Joseph Thoburn, of the Oklahoma Historical Society. The Osage shield is crossed by an Indian peace pipe and a branch of olive which "betoken a predominant love of peace by a united people". The blue field of the flag and the peace pipe are taken from one used earlier by the Choctaw nation. On 9 May 1941 the name of the state was added beneath the central emblems.

The state seal appears in the center of the governor's flag, which is green, and has five stars around the seal. The seal was adopted in 1907 on the basis of one previously designed for the proposed state of Sequoyah. It contains a large white star on a blue field which also contains 45 smaller stars. On the branches of the large star are the emblems of the five Indian nations and in its center is the former seal of Oklahoma Territory, adopted in 1893. This depicts Liberty with a farmer and an Indian and the motto *Labor omnia vincit* ("Work conquers all").

Before 1925 Oklahoma had a flag adopted on 2 March 1911. It was red with a large white blue edged star containing the number 46. Its red field caused it to lose popularity after the Russian Revolution.

History	One of the Great Plains states. Originally part of the Louisiana Purchase, left unorganized as the Indian Territory for many years. After opening up by white settlers it became a regular Territory in 1890; was admitted as a State on 16 November 1907
Area	69,919 sq miles
Population	(1986) 3,305,000
Capital	Oklahoma City
Largest City	Oklahoma City
Major Products	Oil, gas, wheat, timber
State Motto	*Labor omnia vincit* ("Work conquers all")
State Colors	Green and white
Bird	Scissor-tailed Flycatcher
Tree	Redbud
Flower	Mistletoe

OREGON

The Beaver State

Oregon is now the only state to have a double-sided flag, i.e. one with a different design on either side. The obverse has the central part of the seal, all in yellow, with the name above and the date of admission below, whereas the reverse has a beaver standing on its dam, also in yellow. The beaver recalls the fur-trapping industry of former times. The flag was adopted on 26 February 1925, and specifications were issued in 1962 and 1966. The occasion for the adoption of the flag was the same as Alaska's – the need for a flag to display outside the Post Office building in Washington D.C. At first only two flags were made, but the use of it later became more popular and in 1953 state schools and public buildings were required by law to display the flag. Blue and yellow are now the state colors.

The state seal has a shield containing a very complex allegorical landscape showing settlers arriving at the Pacific Ocean, with the motto "The Union" on a scroll. Around the shield are 33 stars, the number of states when Oregon was admitted; the crest is an American eagle with olive branch and arrows, designed by Harvey Gordon and adopted in 1859. A new seal was cut in 1903, in the form which now appears on the flag.

History	The name originally included all the territory that now includes Washington and Idaho, and was once ruled jointly by the U.S.A. and Britain (1818-48). In 1848 it became a Territory in its own right; admitted to the Union on 14 February 1859
Area	97,073 sq miles
Population	(1986) 2,698,000
Capital	Salem
Largest City	Portland
Major Products	Gold and other minerals, cattle, hay, wheat, timber and wood products. Tourism: about 16 million visitors annually
State Motto	The Union
Bird	Western Meadowlark
Tree	Douglas Fir
Flower	Oregon Grape

41

PENNSYLVANIA

The Keystone State

Pennsylvania has a coat of arms as well as a seal. The arms consist of a shield, divided into three parts, one with a ship, one with a plough, and one with three wheatsheaves, all symbolizing the trade and agriculture of the state; the supporters are two horses and the crest is an eagle on a wreath of blue and yellow. Underneath is a scroll with the motto "Virtue, liberty and independence". Only the shield and crest appear on the seal, but the whole arms are portrayed on the flag. The Pennsylvania seal also has a reverse side, one of the few that do, and was created in 1777 and adopted in 1791. The arms were officially adopted in 1809.

The flag was adopted on 13 June 1907, although it had been used previously as the basis for state militia colors. The modern form is based on specifications issued in 1964, which specify that the horses are black, although this makes them very hard to distinguish on a dark blue flag. The governor's flag is like the state flag, but with a white field.

History	Settled in 1682 by Quakers led by William Penn. In the French and Indian War the western part of Pennsylvania was acquired, and Pittsburg founded. Independent government established in September 1776; the state ratified the Constitution on 12 December 1787
Area	45,308 sq miles
Population	(1986) 11,889,000
Capital	Harrisburg
Largest City	Philadelphia ("The City of Brotherly Love")
Major Products	Coal, iron, steel, mushrooms, tobacco, wheat and other cereals
State Motto	Virtue, liberty and independence
Animal	Whitetail Deer (1959)
Bird	Ruffed Grouse (1931)
Tree	Hemlock (1931)
Flower	Mountain Laurel (1933)

RHODE ISLAND

The Little Rhody State

The anchor has always been the heraldic sign for "Hope", and in the case of Rhode Island the two have been together on the seal since 1664, and now appear on the state's coat of arms and flag. During the Revolutionary War the Second Rhode Island Regiment carried a flag with the anchor and motto, and a canton with 13 stars. During the Civil War the central part of the seal was used on a blue flag. In 1881 the arms were officially created by placing the anchor on a blue field. The state adopted a flag on 30 March 1877, with a white field and blue anchor in a red frame within a ring of 38 stars. This was replaced by a second design on 1 February 1882, of blue with the anchor in a red frame within a ring of 13 stars, all yellow. At that time the anchor had a rope around it, but this was removed in 1892 from all the state emblems. On 19 May 1897 the present flag was authorized, which recalls the Regimental Color of 1777.

The governor's flag is white with the state arms in the center and a blue star in each corner. This dates from 21 May 1931. The arms are a blue shield with the anchor, the name of the state in blue letters on a yellow scroll above and the word "Hope" on a scroll below. The state seal is like the one of 1664 except for the rope which no longer "fouls" the anchor. It bears the date 1636, the year Rhode Island and Providence Plantations was founded by Roger Williams.

History	The smallest state of the Union. Settlers came from Massachusetts in search of religious freedom in 1636; obtained a charter in 1663 as the Colony of Rhode Island and Providence Plantations. The state renounced allegiance to Britain on 4 May 1776 only reluctantly joined the Union on 29 May 1790
Area	1,214 sq miles
Population	(1986) 975,000
Capital	Providence
Largest City	Providence
Major Products	Metalware, machinery, jewelry-silverware, transport equipment, fish
State Motto	Hope
Bird	Rhode Island Red
Tree	Maple
Flower	Violet

SOUTH CAROLINA

The Palmetto State

South Carolina's flag goes back to the first years of the Revolutionary War. A blue flag with a white crescent was used by Colonel Moultrie on Fort Johnson, the device being that of the cap badge used by the South Carolina troops. A palmetto tree was added to the flag after the successful defence of the log fort in Charleston Harbour in 1776 because the resilient qualities of the palmetto logs helped to save it from the British bombardment. On 28 January 1861 this design was chosen as the national flag of South Carolina, after its secession from the Union, and has remained the state flag ever since.

However, in the month between secession (20 December 1860) and the final choice of flag, several other designs were brought forward. One of these was an interesting forerunner of the Battle Flag of the Confederacy adopted in September 1861. It was a red flag with a blue cross charged with 15 stars (one for each "slave" state) and the crescent and palmetto in the canton. But the designs which prevailed in South Carolina were ones which gave prominence to the palmetto, which was the badge of the state's troops. The palmetto also appears on the obverse side of the seal adopted in 1776.

History	Permanent settlements began in 1670. From 1719 the colony was a royal province. A council of safety took over in 1775 and the governor fled. Constitution ratified on 23 May 1788; seceded on 20 December 1860; re-admitted in 1868
Area	31,113 sq miles
Population	(1986) 3,376,000
Capital	Columbia
Largest City	Charleston
Major Products	Tobacco, soya beans, corn, non-metallic minerals, cotton and textiles
State Motto	*Dum spiro, spero* ("While I breathe I hope")/*Animas opibusque parati* ("Prepared in soul and resources")
Bird	Carolina Wren
Tree	Palmetto
Flower	Jessamine

SOUTH DAKOTA

The Sunshine State ◇ The Coyote State

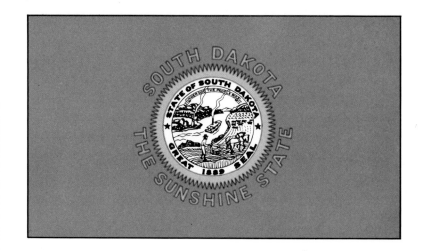

Before 1963 South Dakota had a flag whose obverse side very aptly expressed its nickname, of sky-blue with a large golden sun in the centre with the name and nickname around it. The reverse side had the state seal in dark blue stitching. The original design was the work of the Secretary of the State Historical Society, Doane Robinson, and Senator Ernest May. However, having two designs proved to be awkward and costly, and so the legislature attempted to combine them by placing the seal over the sun on both sides of the flag. This was the work of Will Robinson, son of Doane Robinson, and his successor as Secretary of the Historical Society. This alteration dates from 11 March 1963. The previous design had been adopted on 1 July 1909. Another feature of the 1963 legislation was the failure to specify the color of the circular band around the seal. Legally this can be either white or sky-blue.

The seal dates from 1885 and is another allegorical landscape depicting the industry and agriculture of the state with the motto "Under God the people rule". The date was added when South Dakota became a state and the seal was adopted by the constitution.

History	Part of Dakota Territory from 1861; became a state on 2 November 1889 (the same day as North Dakota). Had been part of French Louisiana; was settled from 1857 onward, as part of Missouri Territory, especially after the Homestead Act of 1863 and the gold strike of 1874
Area	77,116 sq miles
Population	(1986) 708,000
Capital	Pierre
Largest City	Sioux Falls
Major Products	Gold, silver, oats, rye, sunflower seed, processed food
State Motto	Under God the people rule
Animal	Coyote
Bird	Chinese Ringneck Pheasant
Tree	Black Hills Spruce
Flower	Pasque Flower

TENNESSEE

The Volunteer State

Some of the inspiration for the design of the flag of Tennessee comes from the flags of the Confederacy. Its three stars have been given various interpretations, the most likely one being that Tennessee was the third state to join the Union after the original 13. The flag was designed by a captain of the National Guard and officially adopted on 17 April 1905. Tennessee had a previous flag, adopted on 30 April 1897, of red, blue and white diagonal stripes. On the blue was the state nickname "The Volunteer State" in gold, and on the white the number 16 in blue, indicating that Tennessee was the sixteenth state. The flag was designed for the Centennial Exposition of 1897 but was not much used later.

The governor's flag is red with a green hickory bush on a red and white wreath. On the bush are three stars, and in each corner of the flag is another. The hickory commemorates Andrew Jackson ("Old Hickory"), whilst the red and white crest-wreath is in the colors of England from where most early settlers came. The three stars are from the state flag, and the four stars indicate the governor's rank as commander-in-chief. The hickory bush is also the badge of the National Guard. Tennessee also has a seal, adopted in 1801, but it does not appear on any flag.

History	First settled in 1757. The area was recognized as British in 1763. A colonial government was begun in 1772, but was annexed to North Carolina in 1776. It passed to the U.S.A. in 1790; was made a state on 1 June 1796. It seceded on 24 June 1861 and was re-admitted on 24 July 1866
Area	42,144 sq miles
Population	(1986) 4,803,000
Capital	Nashville
Largest City	Memphis
Major Products	Cotton, tobacco, soya beans, wood products, iron and steel, chemicals, synthetic fibres
State Motto	Agriculture and commerce
Bird	Mocking Bird
Tree	Tulip Poplar
Flower	Iris

TEXAS

The Lone Star State

The well-known flag of Texas waved over the area when it was an independent republic, although it was not the first to do so. The first flag of the republic was blue with a large white star and the name Texas between the points. This lasted until December 1836 when one with a plain gold star was adopted. The present flag was adopted on 25 January 1839. It also had a maritime version in which the colors were laid horizontally with the star in the center, and a naval ensign modelled on the Stars and Stripes. The last two went out of use when Texas joined the Union on 29 December 1845. The single star on these flags, which has given Texas its nickname, is thought to have originated in the Bonnie Blue Flag used in West Florida in 1810 (see Mississippi). It is also the only device in the state seal.

The governor's flag is blue with a star in each corner and the central part of the seal in the center. This shows the Lone Star on a light blue disc surrounded by a wreath of olive and oak. The seal dates from 1839, and since 1961 has had a reverse side depicting the coat of arms. These were designed by Mrs. S. Farnsworth and promoted by the Daughters of the American Revolution. On the shield can be seen the Alamo mission, the Gonzales cannon and Vince's Bridge. Around it are the six flags said to have flown over Texas; above is the star and beneath is the motto "Texas One and Indivisible".

History	Texas is the second largest state. It was part of Mexico until 1836 when it was able to secede and form an independent republic, which was admitted to the Union on 29 December 1845. It seceded from the Union on 28 January 1861 and was re-admitted in 1870
Area	266,807 sq miles
Population	(1985) 16,370,000
Capital	Austin
Largest City	Houston
Major Products	Oil, gas, cotton, maize, livestock
State Motto	Friendship
Bird	Mocking Bird (1927)
Tree	Pecan
Flower	Bluebonnet

UTAH

The Beehive State

Utah was settled by the Mormons in 1847. Their emblem was the beehive, and "Deseret", a word meaning honeybee, was the name they gave to their state. It became a Territory of the U.S.A. under the name Utah in 1850. Prior to this a flag like the Stars and Stripes was in use, but in the canton was an eagle grasping a cannon and a beehive, and 14 white stars. In 1851 the canton design was altered to one with the eagle grasping the beehive only and surrounded by the 14 stars. This lasted until 1860 and Utah was then without a flag until 1903 when the Daughters of the American Revolution created one of blue with the central part of the seal (the coat of arms) in white. This was officially adopted on 9 March 1911. On 11 March 1913 the law was altered to allow for the arms to be in color and inside a gold ring.

The seal was adopted in 1850 and contains a coat of arms with a shield depicting a beehive with bees and the word "Industry", together with sego lilies, the state flower. (They commemorate their use as emergency food by the early settlers.) The crest is an American eagle and the shield is flanked by two U.S. flags. The dates are 1847 and 1896.

History	Utah was part of the huge area of Mexico ceded to the U.S.A. in 1848, after being settled by Mormons who founded Salt Lake City. Their state of Deseret was formed in 1849, which became Utah Territory. Mormon polygamy prevented entry to the Union, however, until 4 January 1896
Area	84,899 sq miles
Population	(1985) 1,645,000
Capital	Salt Lake City
Largest City	Salt Lake City
Major Products	Copper, gold, oil, gas, barley, wheat, primary metals, fabricated metals and machinery
State Motto	Industry
Bird	Sea Gull
Tree	Blue Spruce (1933)
Flower	Sego Lily (1911)

VERMONT

The Green Mountain State

The coat of arms of Vermont depicts a pine tree like that of Maine, and dates from 1821. It is based on the seal of 1779, and has the pine tree, cow, wheatsheaves and woodland on an ornate shield. The crest is a stag's head, and the shield is surrounded by pine-branches. A scroll bears the motto "Freedom and unity", also taken from the seal. It is not known if Vermont had a flag during its period of independence (1777-91). It adopted its first flag on 1 May 1804 by adding the state's name to a Stars and Stripes of 17 stripes. On 20 October 1837 it adopted another Stars and Stripes, with a white star in the canton containing the state's coat of arms, but during the Civil War the arms were used on a plain blue flag. On 1 June 1923 it was decided to make such a flag the official state flag.

A much-honored flag in Vermont is the Bennington Battle Flag said to have been carried by the Green Mountain Boys on 16 August 1777. Since 1963 a replica of it is flown annually at the State House on the anniversary of the battle, even though modern scholarship has cast considerable doubts on the validity of the flag. The flag is an early Stars and Stripes with the number 76 set among the stars, and with the order of the white and red stripes reversed.

History	In the centre of Vermont are the Green Mountains that give it its name. It was part of French Canada until 1760, after which it was disputed between New York and New Hampshire. Declared itself independent on 16 January 1777. After the Revolutionary War it was allowed to join the Union, on 4 March 1791
Area	9,614 sq miles
Population	(1986) 541,000
Capital	Montpelier
Largest City	Burlington
Major Products	Dairy produce, hay, fruit, maple syrup, stone, timber, machine tools, electronics
State Motto	Freedom and unity
Bird	Hermit Thrush
Tree	Sugar Maple
Flower	Red Clover

VIRGINIA

The Old Dominion

Virginia's seal tells a story in classical allegorical style. The female figure is Virtus (the "genius" = presiding spirit) of the Commonwealth treading on the body of Tyranny. Virtus is dressed as an Amazon armed with a spear and sword. The tyrant's crown has fallen from his head, and he grasps a chain and a whip. Her victory is emphasized in the motto *Sic semper tyrannis* ("Thus ever to tyrants"). The classical costumes and the motto remind us of the way in which the freed colonies looked to the ancient Roman republic for inspiration. For this reason also many state Capitols are built in the Roman style. The seal is surrounded by a wreath of an unknown plant, possibly a vine. It was designed by George Wythe in 1776, and has a reverse side as well, not used on flags. The seal was more closely defined in 1930.

The seal was placed on a blue flag, in a white disc on 30 April 1861 immediately after the act of secession from the Union. This flag has remained in use ever since, the seal being replaced by the revised one in 1931, and the colors defined in 1949. Traditionally, although not according to any official specifications, the flag has a silver fringe at the flying end.

History	The first chartered settlement was made in Virginia in 1607 at Jamestown. Tobacco was under cultivation by 1619. In 1775 the governor had to step down and in 1781 the British surrendered at Yorktown. Virginia ratified the Constitution on 25 June 1788; seceded on 17 April 1861; was re-admitted on 26 January 1870
Area	40,767 sq miles
Population	(1986) 5,787,000
Capital	Richmond
Largest City	Norfolk
Major Products	Corn, hay, peanuts, tobacco and tobacco products, coal
State Motto	*Sic semper tyrannis* ("Thus ever to tyrants")
Bird	Cardinal
Tree	Flowering Dogwood
Flower	Flowering Dogwood

WASHINGTON

The Evergreen State ◇ The Chinook State

Washington is the only state to have a green flag, commemorating its well-known nickname. Here again the Daughters of the American Revolution were instrumental in getting the flag adopted, pressurizing the legislature to adopt the flag they had designed. This placed the seal in color in the center of the green flag. The flag was authorized on 7 June 1923, after seven years of lobbying. Since then the flag has been slightly revised and regularized by legislation of 1925, 1955 and 1967. According to the 1967 specifications the flag is dark green, in proportions 3:5 with the seal's diameter two-thirds of the width. There may or may not be a gold fringe.

The seal was created in 1889 by Charles Talcott, owner of the store which the legislators visited to have a seal cut. He rejected their over-elaborate design and suggested the present one. The label from a bottle of cough medicine was used to provide a model for the picture of Washington. Prior to this Washington (then a territory) had a seal of the allegorical-landscape type, and can therefore be grateful to Charles Talcott and his brother Grant (who did the artwork) for providing the new state with something more distinctive and memorable.

History	The state lies in the extreme north-east and is the nearest one to Alaska; it shares the Vancouver coastline with British Columbia. It was part of the Oregon Country once shared by Britain and the U.S.A., and became a Territory in its own right in 1853 and a state on 11 November 1889
Area	68,139 sq miles
Population	(1985) 4,409,000
Capital	Olympia
Largest City	Seattle
Major Products	Timber and wood products, wheat, livestock, fish, primary aluminum
State Motto	*Alki* ("By and by")
State Color	Green and gold
Bird	Willow Goldfinch
Tree	Western Hemlock
Flower	Rhododendron

WEST VIRGINIA

The Mountain State

West Virginia has seal and a coat of arms. The arms are now on the flag and are taken from the obverse of the seal, which was adopted in 1863, soon after the formation of the state from those western counties of Virginia that voted against leaving the Union. The boulder in the centre of the emblem carries the date of admission. On a scroll is the state motto *Montani semper liberi* ("Mountain men are always free"). The arms were first placed on a flag on 28 January 1864 when flags were authorized for the state regiments. Then at the time of the Louisiana Purchase Exposition in 1905 a flag was created for the state pavilion. This was white with the arms on one side and a sprig of the "big laurel" (the state flower) on the other, both sides bordered in red and blue. This was legalized on 24 February 1905. At the Jamestown Exposition in 1907 a revised form of it, with the name added on a scroll and the red border removed, was in use.

The present form was authorized on 7 March 1929, and came about as a result of the cost of making double-sided flags, as it now has the same design on both sides. The "big laurel" has been reduced to a wreath around the coat of arms, over which is the name of the state on a red ribbon. The "big laurel" (*Rhododendron maximum*) was adopted as the state flower in 1903.

History	West Virginia was part of Virginia until 1862. After the secession of Virginia the western counties voted to set up a new state, which was admitted to the Union by proclamation on 20 June 1863
Area	24,282 sq miles
Population	(1985) 1,936,000
Capital	Charleston
Largest City	Charleston
Major Products	Coal, oil, gas, hay, corn, tobacco, livestock, primary and fabricated metal, chemicals
State Motto	*Montani semper liberi* ("Mountain men are always free")
Bird	Cardinal
Tree	Sugar Maple
Flower	Rhododendron

WISCONSIN

The Badger State

Many states whose flags are short on distinctive and memorable features have resorted to writing their names on them, and this applies particularly to those which are plain blue fields with seals or coats of arms. Montana and Wisconsin are the latest to take this route. The original flag of Wisconsin was the military Color of blue with the state arms, created on 25 March 1862. At that time the U.S. arms were depicted on the reverse side. This design was allowed to lapse in 1887, but on 29 April 1913 was revived with the state arms on both sides. This remained so until 1980 when the flag was revised to include the name of the state in white block letters above the arms and the date of admission, 1848, below. The flag shape and the design and colors of the arms were also specified in more detail.

The arms and seal were designed by Governor Nelson Dewey and Chief Justice Edward Ryan while they were sitting on the steps of a New York bank in 1851. In their design the allegorical objects are placed in the quarters of a shield which also contains the shield of the U.S.A. within a belt (originally a scroll) with the national motto. The crest is a badger, referring to the state nickname, which came from the burrows like badgers' setts in which the early prospectors used to live. The supporters are a miner and sailor, representing commerce on land and water (the Great Lakes).

History	It was first settled by the French and part of New France until 1763 when it was ceded to Britain. In 1783 Britain conceded it to the U.S.A., and it was part of the North-West Territory until 1836 when it became the Territory of Wisconsin which was admitted to the Union on 29 May 1848
Area	56,154 sq miles
Population	(1987) 4,794,792
Capital	Madison
Largest City	Milwaukee
Major Products	Dairy products, mink, snap beans, hay and corn, timber and wood products, machinery, metalware, processed food, tourism
State Motto	Forward
Bird	Robin
Tree	Sugar Maple
Flower	Wood Violet

WYOMING

The Equality State

Like South Dakota Wyoming has succumbed to the temptation to put its seal on an otherwise highly attractive and symbolic flag. It was designed by Mrs. A. C. Keyes of Buffalo, Wyoming for a competition organized by the Daughters of the American Revolution, and was adopted in this form by the legislature on 31 January 1817. In Mrs. Keyes's design the bison faced the fly, but now it always faces the hoist. The colors are of those of the national flag, and may stand for the Indians, the sacrifices of the pioneers (red), purity and uprightness (white) and the blue of the sky and mountains. The bison was once the "monarch of the plains" where Wyoming is situated.

The seal dates from 1893 but was revised in 1921. It has classical elements similar to those of Virginia. Here the central figure is Victory, flanked by a cowboy and a miner and two columns bearing lamps. Round these are ribbons with the names of the chief products of the state (grain, oil, etc.). On her pedestal is the emblem of the U.S.A. The figure of Victory bears a scroll reading "Equal rights", commemorating the fact that the constitution of Wyoming was the first to give votes to women. She is supposed to be modelled from the well-known statue "The Victory of Samothrace", but in fact is not. The seal on the flag is in black stitching.

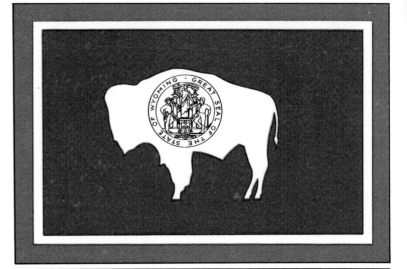

History	The eastern part was once subject to France and the western to Spain (later to Mexico). The U.S. acquired the French territory in 1803 and the Mexican in 1848. Settlers arrived from 1834 onward. A Territory was organized in 1868. It was admitted to the Union on 10 July 1890
Area	97,809 sq miles
Population	(1986) 485,111
Capital	Cheyenne
Largest City	Cheyenne
Major Products	Oil, gas, coal, livestock: Tourism 5 million visitors annually
State Motto	Equal rights
Bird	Meadowlark (1927)
Tree	Cottonwood (1947)
Flower	Indian Paint Brush (1917)